HOW GOOD DO YOU WANT IT!?
(Various Aspects of Your Life)

Developing Positive Mindsets for
Every Day in Every Way!

The Goal of this book is to raise $1,000,000 dollars for local and international charities and plant 100,000 trees on planet Earth!

Edward Michael Raymond
www.Marquis-Motivations.com

Contact the Author @ **EdwardMichaelRaymond@bell.net**
Author Credits: B.A. Philosophy U. of W. Toastmasters ACS

Printed in the United States of America.

ISBN: 978-1-4269-6784-9 (sc)
ISBN: 978-1-4269-6785-6 (hc)
ISBN: 978-1-4269-6786-3 (e)

Library of Congress Control Number: 2011915796

Trafford rev. 09/01/2011

 www.trafford.com

North America & international
toll-free: 1 888 232 4444 (USA & Canada)
phone: 250 383 6864 ♦ fax: 812 355 4082

About the Author

Edward Michael Raymond was born in Windsor, Ontario Canada. He resides in Puce, Ontario with his wife Monica and their three children: Camila, Sarah & Lucas.

He is a graduate from the University of Windsor with a B.A. in philosophy.

Edward has taught and volunteered in Ghana, West Africa, Riobamba, Ecuador, and Cochabamba, Bolivia, in South America.

At present, he is a junior partner at Leisure Trailer Sales, a Family Owned/ Family Driven RV dealership. Sales Manager, Marketer & Trainer

Edward is a Toastmaster CC, ACS, and is a Motivational Speaker.

He is also the founder/creator of www.Marquis-Motivations. com

"All true motivation comes from within the individual." EMR

The "How Good Do You Want It!? (Tm) is a series of transformative writings to inspire and move people forward in a positive and reflective way. It is with the sincerest and most heartfelt hope that this little book will also benefit others on the planet today and tomorrow by sharing the funds generated from its success.

<u>Acknowledgements:</u> To all my friends, coaches, writers, speakers, professors, teachers and students for reading and responding is such a positive, critical way, you will never know how much heartfelt I valued your input.

Blessings upon you all: Becky, Maurice, Melissa, Mony, Paul, Liana, Linda, Prof. MacKendrick, Carol, Scott, Glen, Dude, Shirley, Cathy, Andrew and a whole lot more. Thank you!

A very "Heartfelt" Special Thanks to: Scott Sharp Armstrong www.bouldercoachingacademy.com & Glen Mollet www.winandsucceed.com who both have been pillars on this project.

This first book is dedicated to my wife Monica and all of humanity!

CONTENTS

INTRODUCTION

What motivated me to write this little book? What motivates anybody to do anything?

One day as I was driving down the road to see a possible trade on a RV, I was listening to the radio. We have a family RV business, and I am the guy who usually goes out to view and inspect the trailer to give it a value of worth. I always spent a good amount of time listening to success cds, the news and great songs on the radio.

At the time I was carrying a boat load of debt along with millions of others within the "credit made easy phenomena" around the globe.

The commercial on the radio indicated "how to get out of debt" it got my attention.

I wrote down the number and couldn't wait to get back to the office and call the number.

Sound familiar?

With eager anticipation I called the number, I thought this is my window of opportunity. "I'm sorry sir; this programme is only available in the United States"

We live close to the U.S. border, Windsor, Ontario is a sister city to Detroit and we pick up a lot of the great radio stations on both sides of one of the friendliest international borders in the world.

The lady on the phone was very pleasant, we spoke for a short period of time and then she referred me Conant-Knightgale's web site. She mentioned, I might be able to find something worthwhile there to consider! Consider! Jackpot! It is an awesome site filled with contacts, coaches, programmes and everything under the sun in the field of "personal-development" success stuff and more. I do a lot of reading in those areas to begin with anyways, and I think, "Our world could always use another positive message and love song"

I came across an organization that offered some "coaching" towards goals and making things happen in your life. Through Mike Litman's organization, I became very good friends with a Mr. Scott Armstrong who runs his own Bolder Coaching Academy and has stayed with my progress as a true friend. The number of people who come in and out of your life can be abundant; however, the ones that stay the course with you in times of doubt, struggle and progress are the ones that really enrich your life, if you are open to developing yourself, personally.

Here are some of the ideas, reflections and ponderings I use and believe in to keep myself moving forward. Some of the concepts might appear to be repetitive, please note that is my intention. I don't know about you, but sometimes I need an idea to be repeated a few times before it really sinks in and sticks.

Here we go!

It is better to be and see, all that can possibly be imagined and experienced, than just wondering, what could have been in my life.

Everything matters, everything counts, and everything happens for a reason, whether we realize it or not at the time we are experiencing it.

Really, it's up to you! The choice is yours, even if you choose not to be all that you are pre-gifted to be, you are making a choice, right? Think about it.

Every day, in every way, we are, what we have been thinking about to a greater or lesser extent. Yesterday, today and tomorrow, we are all thinking and moving towards what we really want to become. Are we doing it by conscious choice or just going through the motions of our day, by default?

However you want to look at it, think about it: however you want to be, act, or create, the fact is we are in an ocean of constant motion.

The fact is life is ongoing, in the good, the bad and the ugly. Life is in the explainable, the un-explainable, in the mystery, mystic or misery, in the bounty, the beautiful, and the beliefs of so many. The universe is constantly expanding. Are you, and I don't mean at the waistline either?

Stop waiting, whining and wishing it was all different. You were different, you are unique.

Make the difference, be the difference.

M. Ghandi: *"Be the difference you want in the world."*

This book will examine some ideas and ask a lot of questions that make us think about our future in a progressive way.

All the questions put forth are designed to help one reflect, ponder, and hopefully move oneself in a forward manner. This is my humble intention.

The more we stop and think about the obvious and the subtle reality in a progressive way, I remain optimistic, the better we can understand, enhance and truly live our lives in the moment.

Think about 3 things that you would like to be different in *your life.*

"Just Do It" - **Nike**
1) _____
2) _____
3) _____

The human brain is more complex than any super computer invented. You are one of the highest forms of creation on the planet. Here is a surprise.
You are a vessel! You have a purpose! You have a reason for being here!
Life is a wonderful mystery, constantly unfolding and continually coming into being, existing and expanding!   *How Good Do You Want it my amigo?*

You are more in control than you might realize, or give yourself credit for.
Stop being an *extra* in your own life, this is not a dress rehearsal.
The picture you constantly create in your mind will be played out.

For everyone who holds this book in their hands, reads it from a computer screen or listens to it, please know that I am like you. There are times I'm waiting, wondering, watching and trying to make sense of life, things, situations and world events. I'm always questioning, why do people do the things they do, why can't everyone just get along, from friends, family, neighbors, nations, whiners, winners and everyday people? We all need each other to grow, sustain, build up ourselves, our nations and look at all the great things people have done and created over the centuries.

How good do we all really want it; our lives, today, tomorrow and together?

What are we all doing? Have you ever really stopped and thought about it?
What am I trading the days, hours, minutes and seconds of my life for, really and truly?
Will it really matter a hundred years from now to anyone, what any of my so called petty problems are currently, and making me so upset right now?
Why am I losing time, effort and energy over something that is non-essential or doesn't really add value to my life, the way I truly want it be?

Am I taking my life to the 100% accountability and responsibility level?

Do you blame your parents, your family, your friends, your community, your government, your nation, and your neighbors for all the results, your feelings, and your attitudes about life in general? Do you complain about circumstances, or do you look for the circumstances you want?

Am I a blamer? What am I?
Only you can answer that for yourself.

I believe all the answers are here for us.

It is our level of awareness and understanding that has to be continually developed and constantly expanded, ideally every day, in every way, every time, with an earnest effort. Is it easier said then done, my friend? Is it?

Do you live your life by default by just going through the motions, day in, day out, or do you consciously choose to leave your comfort zone and consciously choose what to think?
How do you do something, how do you proceed with a clarity that resonates with your sense of purpose and being? These are worthwhile questions for they can yield definite results.

Do you live your life on purpose, with a purpose, or do you adopt a pessimistic world view and blindly accept that you cannot change your life and world?
Do you live your life by design or default? Are they your designs or someone else's?

The choice is yours, *every day.*

Think about it, this is your life; you're the master maker, putting the pieces together.
Is your life the masterpiece of your doing?

How Good Do You Want IT!?

Do you know the difference between the brain and the mind?
Think about it for a moment. *Mind   Brain*
There is more to life than meets the eye.

How healthy do you want to be?
How wealthy do you want to be?
How successful do you want to be?

How rich do you want your life to be on every level and in every dimension?

How Good Do You Want it all to Be?

Positive Points to Ponder:

If I am the master of my destiny, when do I finally get crystal clear on every aspect of my Life?

What are the primary areas I really need to focus on right now?

By taking action now in one area of my life, then moving onto another, I can make the difference, the change, the new attitude of gratitude for everything that I have going for me now, today, even I am living under a bridge and sleeping on a park bench.

List 3 things I have going for me in my favor:
1) _____
2) _____
3) _____

Your thought notes:
_____
_____
_____
_____
_____
_____
_____
_____
_____
_____

CHAPTER 1

First Thoughts

At this point, I would like to formally define some words from Webster's New Collegiate Dictionary

These concepts are as follows:

The Brain:
the portion of the vertebrate central nervous system that constitutes the organ of thought and neural coordination, includes all the higher nervous centers receiving stimuli, from the sense organs and interpreting and correlating them to formulate the motor impulses, is made of neurons and supporting and nutritive structures, is enclosed within the skull, and is continuous with the spinal cord through the foramen magnum.

The Mind:
The element or complex of elements in an individual that feels, perceives, thinks, wills, and especially reasons. The conscious mental events and capabilities in an organism. The organized conscious and unconscious adaptive mental activities of an organism. You☺

Be mindful of some key words in the definition of mind, pun intended.

Conscious:

1) *sharing another's knowledge or awareness of an inward state or outward fact.*
2) *perceiving, apprehending, or noticing with a degree of controlled thought or observation.*

Consciousness:

1   a: *the quality or state of being aware especially of something within oneself*
    b: *the state or fact of being conscious of an external object, state or fact*
    c: *concern, awareness*
2: *the state of being characterized by sensation, emotion, volition, and thought Mind*
3: *the totality of conscious states of an individual*
4: *the normal state of conscious life*
5: *the upper level of mental life of which the person is aware as contrasted with the unconscious processes*

Subconscious:

1: *existing in the mind but not immediately available to consciousness*
2: *imperfectly or incompletely conscious, the mental activities just below the threshold of consciousness*

Paradigm:

A paradigm is defined as an example, pattern, especially an outstandingly clear or typical example.
The archetype is an original pattern or model of which all things of the same type are representations or copies of that idea.

I put these definitions intentional in the beginning just to kick start this reflective read. You will see its worth and just start thinking about, how I am coming to understand myself just a little bit better. I know when we feel uncomfortable at times, don't fully understand some things, we hit this terror barrier and we wonder what we are doing. This is OK to feel uncomfortable; you are shifting a level of awareness. We are all constantly exposed to, marketed to, programmed to think, buy and sell in a certain kind of way. Step back, step out and free think for a moment. How am I really thinking about what is going on around me? Ask yourself, why do I think that way at times?

We think in paradigms, our actions are running on paradigms whether we realize this or not.
We keep getting the same results but what we have been accustomed to thinking in a certain kind of way, right?

Positive point to ponder!
Am I taking 100% responsibility for all the results I am getting in my life?

Physically, Emotionally, Intellectually, Spiritually

Is it my environment, my parents, my job, my government, my economy, my nation and or my cultural conditioning that have led me up to where I am today?
How did I get to be where I am today and why are other people where they are?
Do I ever really stop and think about that? Do I ask those kinds of questions, do I want to, have to, should I? Why bother?

"Oh well, just another day, I'll play along, see how it goes, that's just the way it is.
I really long for something better, maybe later, maybe another day, another time.

Maybe my luck might change. It is what it is."
Does any of that sound familiar, can I relate to it?
I can, I have, I did, and sometimes I still do!

Hold the phone! Stop right there!

Do you really think that's the way it is, has to be, meant to be?
Am I taking 100% responsibility for all the results I'm getting? Am I taking 100% responsibility for the way I'm feeling, everyday in everyway?
Am I choosing to live the life I want by design, my designs or just by default of seeing how the next twenty-four hours turn out?

Key everyday thought!

My life, by my designs, my reality intentionally created on purpose.

Napoleon Hill states in his book: **Think and Grow Rich,** states about reality: "Not in an instant, but in a continuous flow of form, persistence of action towards it."   This is great food for thought on how we continuously think about something, engage our mind towards it, to start to bring in about in our daily lives. The daily discipline towards achieving a goal, we desire with an earnest effort.

The Key is *action* always towards that which you desire. How do you want it to be?

Do you think Walt Disney gave up when someone didn't believe in his ideas, his dreams, his magic Kingdom, his imaginary figures? We are still experiencing his dream works today!

Did Fred Smith creator of FedEx give up on his idea of an overnight letter for a few bucks more than regular postage and look at that company today.

Some times, you have to be your own best friend, *believe to achieve*. It doesn't matter where you are coming from, what has happened to you last year, last month, last week, yesterday, 10 minutes ago. All that matters is right now, today this very moment and where you are going.

You have 86,400 seconds in a day, make each one count, they are yours! Am I moving myself "towards a progressive realization of a worthy ideal or goal(s)" **Earl Nightingale's** famous quote. What about my health, wealth, success, relationships, friendships, business or where ever I find myself right now today? Even if you are not exactly where you want to be, struggling with tough circumstances, its ok, the time to change is always ready for you today, right now. Make all aspects of your actions in your life count, isn't it worth it, every day in every way?

Make a short concise list of anything you want in your life. Check back on your previous list; are there any changes that need to be made so the two lists become consistent with each other?
Is your thinking in align with the changes and things you want in your life?

1) _____
2) _____
3) _____

Every day, do 1, 2, 3 action steps towards one of the goals you picked, or all three. If you only do 1 today, that's OK! If you do 3, right on! If you do 10 for each or more, more power to you!

Accomplishing anything action oriented builds up self-esteem and self confidence every time, every day. No matter how big or how small the accomplishment, it does, it builds you up.

Keep moving forward.

"Press on" has solved more problems, dilemmas, sticky situations, and will always seize the day.

Make it count. *"Everything Counts."* **Brian Tracy - The Great American Business Coach**

We all have made mistakes, messed up, missed the ball, struck out, put our foot in our mouth, over spent, mismanaged, badly budgeted, and said something we regretted.

Should've, would've, could've. We all have a collective past. We lived, learned, are living are learning and are now moving on. The past is the past and cannot be changed. Stop worrying about it. OK, here you are. What is done is done, said is said. It can't be erased; it's in the memory bank, a good reference point for present and future living decisions, right? Today is the day, your day. Every decision you make moves you forward or backwards. The choice is constantly yours. The future is out there, yet to be imagined, created, and in faith, thought about it. What we do today plants seeds towards what will be in the future. A fine notion some may say. What you do, eat, drink, and think about does get reflected a bit into tomorrow, and would you agree?

This life is not a one act play. What you have is the *now*. By being fully engaged and present with your family, friends and at work, makes the day all the more worthwhile. What you do right now and think about counts, it is important. It's all important.

One day when I wanted to transfer a course credit from college to university, I went into the office of the register to see about transferring this course and the fellow student looked at me and said; "sorry it doesn't count" I just smiled and walked away, yes every thing in my life counts! ☺

Right now, is the moment!

How are you talking to yourself? How do you feel? How you interpret what others say and do has to be filtered through your own perceptions of what counts and matters in your life.

Are you aware of your thinking, your thoughts, the actions you make, take?

Are you consciously aware of your thoughts, what you are thinking about, bringing about? Ask yourself am I thinking good things, great things, "what could be things", what if things?

Am I thinking life giving, selfish living, or always giving?

The choice is yours, every day in every way!

Canadian Rock Band **RUSH** from the song **Freewill:** *"If you choose not to decide, you still have made a choice."*

Positive points to ponder:
How much do you value your own personal thoughts over someone else's thoughts about what you're doing in your own life?

Your thoughts are paramount to the life you want to create, today and for tomorrow.

Thoughtful Notes By You:

_____

_____

_____

_____

_____

_____

_____

_____

CHAPTER 2

Action - Attitude - Alignment

Always try to have the right attitude, a good attitude a more positive attitude. Well, what is the right attitude? Two people can be playing a sport, one very focused, one very relaxed, both play exceptionally well. They both have the right attitude towards the game. Your right attitude is determined by you. How you respond to a situation and how it positively affects those around you will be a good indicator of how good is your right attitude. You are responsible 100% of the time for your attitude, and for the actions you take today and tomorrow.

I believe the more we are stretching ourselves, challenging our thinking, our notions, and shifting the paradigms we are operating on, the greater our clarity becomes. Most of our attitude will dictate a significant response, we receive from other people.

When I go to work and be with other people, my personal attitude reflects how they respond to me.
If I am doing my best, giving an earnest effort, they pick up on a positive vibration of how I am feeling. Likewise when I am down, have concerned look on my face, they sense that as well. It is my

own attitude at the time. You have ultimate freedom of your own thoughts and attitude to any situation in your life at any given time. Wearing your emotions on your sleeve is OK, but it is better to have your heart out there and in every thing you do as well, I think.

A true sense of direction and purpose will begin to unfold and reveal itself all along the way when we are become more aware of what we are truly capable of becoming.

This gift, a realized awareness, assists us to become more of who we are meant to be.

It all begins with our right thinking, a right attitude and having an attitude of constant gratitude is paramount to move us forward. If you want more, think and be thankful more for every thing you do have, right now in this moment. It is in the appreciating what do have. ☺

How fast we want to move forward is entirely up to us. The universe moves quickly, do you?

How best am I utilizing my time? Are my thoughts and actions moving me forward, or am I just going through the motions?

Everything and everyone has a rhythm whether of slow, fast, creative, stagnant or not. Are you one force moving upon another force in your life to create the circumstances you want?

By continuing our conscious awareness this helps us to handle our happiness, to move ourselves, our lives forward, faster, frequently, forever.

All movement towards a goal, an object of your desire, a dream to have come true, a relationship sought after, comes from a deep down desire inside of you. Desire is the first spark of that idea to want to change something. That great idea, that paradigm of your definiteness of purpose is paramount to you to make it all worthwhile: Your life.

Desire is the beginning movement, an inclination towards action.

That desire, maybe a flicker, maybe a flash of imagination that leads to a "what if" scenario.

I want that! I could do that! I want to be that or better! You can be anything you want to be, if you have the will to do it.

We are continually shaping our minds and the reality of our lives, by the thoughts, images and ideas we have about ourselves, both inner and outer. When we begin to work on ourselves for the better, I believe we see the world and the people in it for the better as well.

How good do you want to see the world to be?

Whether you believe or agree with, one of the universal laws is *the law of cause and effect.* It has an impact on our lives we can't deny. For every action there is a reaction. For everything that has happened, something caused it to happen.

The faculty of belief.

What do you believe, really believe in, in your reality, circumstances and purpose?

What I usually believe to be my reality, circumstances, and situations usually happen or come about, just as expected to a greater or lesser extent.

My belief begins to come true when I believe it enough, would you agree?

Can you relate to that statement? I think we all can to a greater or lesser degree.

"That's always been my belief." How great do you believe yourself to be, how limitless, how do you want to be, really and truly? Am I operating at the highest, grandest vision and belief of my self? Do I think like that, every day in every way, or just sometimes, do I get a glimpse of my ideal self, once in a while, of how I would really like to truly be?

Why can't we maintain that constant awareness every day? Look at our daily efforts, daily actions, how consistent are they with our ideal self?

What attitude of belief do I have? How do I picture myself? Is my attitude my own, or is it a culmination of opinions and thoughts I have taken in by others? We are constantly exposed to others thoughts, opinions and statements about things and events.

The next time you are with someone and general statements are being made based on opinions, ask that person: "How so, is that an actual fact or are you just saying that based on someone else's opinion?" When you ask for the truth, with sincerity, it is amazing how discussions get focused real quickly.

You attitude my friend is a powerful key, to many mysteries in the world.

He or She has a bad attitude, we have all heard that many times. They have a great attitude. Why? Why do I think that way? Why do they think that way? Do I have an attitude of more gratitude?

The best attitude is one of gratitude in every way, everyday, no exceptions.

If I have the right attitude, right thinking, and right words about everything I do, it would stand to reason, my belief, my actions my opportunities would begin to attract and warrant the right circumstances, right? If I am trying, to be the best person I can be every day in every way, and putting forth my best, wouldn't the best come looking for me? *Like attracts like, right?*

To step up one's awareness, and feel the vibration of life, the choice is yours. It always has been and always will be! We all have ups and downs, highs and lows, emotional rollercoaster rides, everyone, that's life!

My friends in Ghana, West Africa, have a saying painted on some of their buses, *"no condition is permanent"* How do we change the conditions and circumstances in our daily lives? How easy it is to truly change one's attitude in an instant: self talk, self thought, a quick mental self guidance of positive belief are the keys.

Alignment

What are the right elements of "who" I am becoming? Are all my attitudes right, about myself? Am I aligning myself in the direction I want to be, or what I think somebody else wants me to be?

How much time do you spend during the day wondering and thinking about what others think about you?
If you only knew how little family, friends and fellow co-workers actually think about you truly during the day, you might honestly be surprised.

SO, whose thoughts matter most to you? Yours. Every day in every way.
How good are you at thinking about yourself, your situation, and your challenges?
Create the circumstances you want to achieve, one step at a time, one action in the direction you want to align yourself towards the good you want in your life and those around you.

Stop and think about, how you're thinking about yourself in regards to any skill you might have or on any level? We all have a personal self-concept about ourselves, in every aspect; how we look, how we dance, how we drive, how we write, speak, do our jobs, we might not actually consciously think about it every day, but it is there and we do.
Are we really in tune and aligned with who we actually are, would like to be or trying to be, want to be? Are you totally happy with whom you are?

It's OK to be in a constant process of becoming! Life is a journey, an incredible experience on many levels. Physical, intellectual, emotional, spiritual. We are just not triune beings.

Action.

The biggest, best, boldest **Key** to which we can unlock every idea, desire, and dream is action. Action is the potion, the elixir, the catalyst, the nexus and the movement of energy from one form to another. The universe lives, breathes, demonstrates action in its ethers, earth, air, water, fire and fusion. All is moved, moving and maintaining via action in some form or another. Amazing isn't it, ask any scientist, just look around. (☺)

How much action are you putting into every aspect of your life? How much action do you want? (Pun intended)
Action is dynamite. If my life is meant to be, more than what it is presently, I, myself, must take action towards changing it, today, tonight, tomorrow! Dance here with me for a moment. My actions or inactions will influence every aspect of my life. You live by your actions. Your mind and body reflect your inner active thoughts. The mental actions within are reflected outward.

What 3 Actions steps am I taking to today to move myself, my life, my goals forward?

Think it, and then ink it!
1) _____
2) _____
3) _____

Action Notes:
_____
_____
_____
_____
_____
_____
_____
_____

CHAPTER 3

Culture   Conditioning   Clarity

Culture can be thought of as people's habits, beliefs, and patterns of group behavior accepted over time from years to decades and even centuries. Most cultures have diverse expressions of life.
How *good* has it been; some great, some not so great even unto today.

How good have we made life on this planet collectively? How Good Do We All want it to be?

There are a lot of things we believe, do and have done in our lives. The sooner we realize, they are part of our culture conditioning, and personal programming to a greater or lesser extent, the better, even all the good, the bad and the ugly. The more aware you become of this conditioning or programming by practice, the sooner you can become aware of how to change unwanted conditioning in your life. We are all creatures of habits. We replace old habits with new habits. Any habit you have that doesn't move you forward or is not life enhancing, might be a habit worthwhile replacing.

Are my daily actions, in constant alignment with what I really want?

I know I should eat better, exercise more, and drink more water. I want what is best for my personhood. Do I really want to be in better shape, to watch, monitor and control what I eat and drink?

How come, I am exactly where I am today with these circumstances, these situations, these challenges in my present life? I am but a cumulative summation of all the choices I have made thus far in my own personal life. Ruts and routines are habits that are hazardous or hectic.

You can change any habit, rut or routine by consciously choosing to replace it with another habit or defined routine that is better or healthier.

There are some things we will always have to do, getting up in the morning, brushing our teeth, driving the kids to school, going to work, preparing meals, every day. Instead of doing the same routine, spice it up a bit. Do them different. Jazz it up! It's your life; you control the routine, the result. Get out of bed on the other side, brush your teeth in the shower or at the kitchen sink and take a different direction to work. Listen to something totally different, opposite of what you like, once in a while. Listen to the radio in another language, prepare a meal you have never made before. Turn off the T.V. for a day!   Try it, you might like it!

There is always hope. When we really stop and think about some of our habits, there are some, we would all like to change. Start of with one, change it or eliminate it, if it doesn't serve your higher purpose.

Try and get out of your comfort zone. Break the routines you've been living in and living out.

Do your habits drain you or develop you?

This is your life, your time! Be a designer habit maker, by your choosing, not by defaulting to the same conditioned way. You make the choice, the difference, the fun, it's worth it.

Why are old habits so difficult to change? Why do new habits warrant more discipline to create? This leads us back to paradigms. Habits are engrained in paradigms of built up experiences and programming. If the habit is strong, the paradigm is well formed. So, we begin through our awareness to see that a paradigm shift is needed. We need to replace the old unhealthy habit with a new one.

Good habits take longer to develop, and bad habits, seem to take root easily.
Why is that?
A good habit takes time to develop, it becomes strong then stronger, and it builds with discipline. "Ah, *discipline*" - is an order of self control, a control gained by consciously enforcing a desired result in whatever field of endeavor.

A bad habit, on the other hand, is quickly developed because it seeks the path of least resistance, instant gratification, almost like an addiction. Interesting, how lots of really bad habits are addictions in some form or another, it seeks a desired effect, usually quickly. Healthy or not.
Our habits are embedded in our paradigms. Our paradigms can have a mixture of both good and bad habits, that's why we can do something or act a certain way one day with such self-control, and the next time, the bad habit takes its' turn.
The more we re-enforce the good habit, the stronger it will become and eventually force out or minimize the bad habit. The more the paradigm is shifted to the "stronger habit," notice I said stronger habit; the more the paradigm will run and play out the results.

The results you are constantly getting in your life are from your paradigms and habits being played out. "*We are creatures of habit*." The greater awareness of this fact is paramount to start changing your results.

Some call this a vibration: *"Higher the vibration, better the results!"*
Bob Proctor

I want to get better and different results in my life. Am I aligning myself with newer, better habits towards that aim?
Do I have an attitude of constant gratitude; am I grateful for everything in my life?
Am I acting consciously or am I re-acting to whatever, whoever comes my way?
Am I living my life by design or default, good enough or just going through the motions?
We live in a world, a universe of constant motion. Are you acting in it, and I don't mean being an "extra" in your own life?
You are the main character. Really, how good do you want every aspect of your life to be?
Am I creating results, the results I truly desire, or am I creating excuses, complaining or compensating?
I have always noticed the people who complain the most about everything are the same ones who don't always appreciate what they have in their life, nor have what they really want in their lives as well.
Conscious gratefulness is one of the key steps to developing a positive mindset amongst the negativity that is all around us.

Clarity

Start right now by becoming aware of your thinking. You are a thinking individual, with the same potential, as anybody else on the planet. How am I thinking about what is happening to me in my life at present? Do I like that feeling, that emotion? Can I improve it, my condition, and my circumstances?

Yes you can! Is my life by my design or someone else's?

If I don't like or really care for my present results or situations, am I taking on the necessary responsibility to change them or make a difference?

Am I waiting for someone to do it for me? If I am, and I don't care for the change or the results, what was I honestly expecting? If I find myself waiting for that someone or something, what happens if they never show up?

Become clear, on your goals and the circumstances you want. Make the changes necessary to obtain what you really want.

Key - New habits can get new results, maybe not in an instant, however, please remember, it is an ongoing process. Creating is a process of constant change. Remember we are human beings, not just human doings!

Just Goal for it!
List here 3 Great BIG Goals you want in your life?
1) _____
2) _____
3) _____

It's up to You!   Today and for tomorrow

In regards to one's **health and eating habits**, we all know what we really need to do: eat less and eat the right kind of foods, plus exercise more. *"Moderation in all things"* **Aristotle: the Greek philosopher.**

Exercise more, sleep enough, and be more active and creative, be less selfish and assist others.

Are you a giver or receiver, taker or provider? Your actions, habits and results reflect that last question. You have a lot more control and self discipline, whether you realize it or not.

Eat healthy, eat happy, and eat the right foods everyday.

Take time when you eat. Eat when you're hungry, not by conditioned timings.

Harmonize eating with others as often and as best as you can. How good do I want my health to be? Exercise leads to good health.

My goals are in the Health Aspect of my Life are as follows:

I want to release _____ pounds from my body.
My ideal weight for me is: _____.
I am affirming and achieving my ideal weight.
I practice envisioning myself at my ideal weight.

KEY: positive affirmations are in the "**I am**" statements, and "**I weigh**" statements are powerful tools that you can use to stay on track.

Positive self talk will go a lot further, than any negative self talk.
If you are going to talk to yourself, (which we are do internally, in one form or another) make it the best, health conscious, smartest, and most successful in any and all endeavors you desire.

You are one of the greatest creations of the universe.
One must continually think and realize that there is no "lack" in the world.
What I mean by that is: all things in existence and created here, come from the four elements on the planet which is part of the infinite universe.
All things created by women, men and children come from the four elements of the earth in some combined form: Earth, Air, Water and Fire. We are connected to the earth and have a vested interest in its healthiness as much as our own. Being green and more sustainable is a must for our present generations as well as for future generations. We all live for today while being mindful for our tomorrows.

Think about how much natural earth we have, the air we breathe, the water around us, the heat/energy amongst us!

What do we do? How do we create? Why do we do, build, make, grow, and produce what we do?

Our ideas over the centuries have been and still are unique, strong and powerful.

Every person born on the planet has the same mind/potential same capabilities, their mind resources, no more or no less, than anyone else.

Isn't that a refreshing thought? We have the same faculties of mind like the "Greats" of times past and present: Socrates, Aristotle, Mozart, Einstein, Newton, Mother Teresa, Trump, Oprah, Gates, and Pope John Paul II, just to name a few:

Your Name Here: (☺)_____

What is greatness, than another form of "***awareness?***"

Bob Proctor: "*The only difference between people is their level of awareness and the results they are getting in their lives.*"

Positive point to ponder:
All true knowledge, true happiness comes from a greater level of awareness. The more understanding you become, the greater the awareness you have in different aspects of your life.

I am writing this book to help me out of my own ignorance of something I've never done before. I am developing another unique awareness of an idea, of how to do something, become more aware, develop myself, so I can have a greater experience(s) of myself, of people, places, situations, of realities and results, I've never had before. To create and to share is an experience that awaits us all, if so inclined.

It's all good!

The continuation of worthy ideals to be pursued every day in every way is paramount to your health, happiness and sense of purpose.

Make the habit of doing and being the person you truly desire to be.

Not, I'll start on Monday. I will start tomorrow. I'll make the changes on the next time, next week, next month or next year.

Start today! Start right now. This is your life. Who is the "author of your life?"

"Be" by intent in every thought, every step. Every action has to be by the right intention of how good do you want it!? How rich do you want it? How wonderful do you want it? How loving, how forgiving do you want it!?

It's not always easy, I know that; consistently thinking about, "how good do I want my body, my mind, my attitude towards everything." How am I emotionally, physically, intellectually, spiritually, in all my relationships with family, friends and foes?

The more you become conscious of your thoughts, (which you have complete control over), your personal power, your expectancy of belief, and *"if it's meant to be, it's really up to me" philosophy, the better.*

How good do you want to be in all areas of your life, is a tall order, and is it attainable?

Just Be It!

To know, is to grow, and the responsibility of it all are now! You are aware!

We always have to have the right attitude, 100% of the time, ideally.

Here is one way of looking at the Right Attitude. ☺

The right attitude: if a =1, b=2 , c=3, d=4 and so on and so forth. When you spell the word ***attitude*** = 100. Nice coincidence, wouldn't you agree?

All movement towards a goal, an objective desired for, a relationship sought after comes from a deep down desire. Again, desire is the beginning movement, inclination towards action.
The flash of an inspiration, that flicker of the imagination, that what if scenario.
I want that. I could be that. I want to be like that, but uniquely myself.

We are continually shaping our minds, bodies, and the reality of ourselves by the thoughts, images, and the ideas we have of ourselves both inner and outer.
How good do you want to be?

The Law of Belief: we can have beliefs right or wrong, different or indifferent. What we continually believe about ourselves usually gets maintained and manifested, and we present it to the world. How are you presenting yourself lately, exactly as you want to, every day in every way? If not, why not?

The Law of Expectancy: if you expect, think, intend, suppose, and anticipate the coming of an occurrence of an event or situation, odds are pretty good you get what you expect.
"It was everything I expected" or ***"that's not what I was expecting."***
It works both ways, like a lot of intentions. What did you expect?
☺

The Law of Attraction: The law of attraction is the buzz of late; actually it has always been in existence. How we understand it, and come to apply it for the betterment of one's life in a form that is life enhancing is always a challenge.

Think it, emotionalize it, and be grateful for it, and all aspects of your life will be played according to laws of motion, physics, beliefs, expectancies, vibrations and attraction. What do you really and truly want for your life? An accumulation of things that will rust into dust, does it really matter 100 years from now, what you drove, where you slept, how much money you earned? Is your legacy in the lives of your family, friends, humanity, is the world a better place because of you? Did you leave someone else better, happier, healthier, and humanity more harmoniously?

It's really up to you. How good do you want to be the "change" in the world?

The world needs you to be your best today and tomorrow.

Are in tune with the laws of the universe? The universe vibrates, higher the vibration, the lighter the frequency of being in tune with it. Are you in tune with the natural rhythm of the way you feel? Do you live a life by your intentional design and do you influence yourself and others in a positive way?

By becoming more aware of your state of affairs, vibrations, correspondences, expectancies, attractions is one of the first big steps, of living a Life you want, not what your parents, your siblings want, or what you think other people want of you, but what you want.

Know what you really want? Think about that for a bit everyday. Write it out.

Is this my best day ever? Did I really milk this day and gave it my all?

Key Question:

What do you have absolute control over?.........*Your Thoughts!*

The way you think about things, the way you feel about things, the way you talk to yourself, internally and externally.

Do you feel like changing anything on your list here now?
What do I really want for my Life?
1) _____
2) _____
3) _____

You are in control. You have the control.
How good do you want that control?
It's your life, by your intentions, are they by design?
Are you living by your will power?
Really stop and think about that.

Positive point to ponder!

My mind, my thoughts, my ideas, my design = my direction towards my destiny.

You know, a whole lot of people think about what other people might be thinking about them, or saying. They worry about what someone else may say about them.
Whose thoughts are more important, yours or theirs?
Whose life are you living yours, or theirs?
How much time do you honestly, constantly think about other people?
Most people are so caught up in their own concerns, petty worries, and some do fall into the trap of thinking about *"what are people thinking or saying about them"*
Your ideas, your thoughts are paramount to your life - creating reality.
Thoughts are one of the purest forms of energy.
*"**Value your thoughts, treasure them**"* Realize that thoughts are neither good nor bad in themselves, objectively.

When you emotionalize and internalize the constant visualization of your thoughts, it has a powerful effect. This thinking from your conscious mind to your subconscious mind activates the vibrations and begins the attractions towards the reality to appear the way you visualized it, eventually. Good, bad and indifferent, we are always experiencing layers of what we have been thinking about. Stop and think about the way the world is right now. Why is it of such great wonders and harsh realities co-existing at the same time? How are the masses of people thinking?

The words we use to describe our reality are very important to maintain and be consistent with the view of the world and our lives we aspire to be and experience.

How you think about things continually defines your perceptions of reality.
Here is a simple example.

Two workers building a bridge both asked the same question.
What are you doing?
1st worker answers; I'm welding steel together to make this bridge. (Correct answer)
2nd Worker: I'm working on this bridge that will connect two nations together and transport millions of people to see each others' great countries. (Correct answer)

Are you a brick layer or building a cathedral?
Are you plucking a string on an instrument or part of a symphony?
Are you making sandwiches for lunch or feeding a family?
Are you just selling something or are you an integral part of a dynamic sales force, that creates products to better our lives, employs hundreds of people from around the world that all benefit from it?
Are you teaching a lesson or transforming minds to think on their own and (for example) find new cures, develop new technologies?
Your mind, your willpower is at your control, right now, today and tomorrow.

Positive Point to Ponder:
One of the greatest gifts of being human is the freedom to have absolute control over our thinking, attitude and choice towards action.

The more you become aware of this fact, the sooner, and the better to start making a difference in the world which you are an integral and well deserving part of life.

Be smart. Be a filter of what you allow into your thinking mind by what, whom, how and when.
Everything counts, everything can make an impression. What are you allowing to be impressed upon you and for how long?

Having the right attitude is a choice, a **habit.**

Habit: *the prevailing disposition or character of a person's thoughts and feelings.*
- *mental make up, settled tendency or usual manner of behavior*
- *a behavior pattern acquired by frequent repetition or physiologic exposure that shows itself in regularity or increased facility of performance.*
- *an acquired mode of behavior that has become nearly or completely involuntary.*
- *addiction.*

What habits do you have that are moving your life forward?
If we are all creatures of habits, how good are your habits?
Do you have any habits that are holding you back, or any feelings you don't have any control over?
Well, actually, you have more control and will power than you might realize.
Any habit good or bad can be replaced by a better or more constructive habit over time. Fact.

Let's get back to attitude as a habit.

Every day in every way we have a choice to choose our attitude to any particular situation.

Lose the old thinking right now of "*that's how I've always been*".

That may be a past fact, however, start erasing the recording, the past programming, the conditioning from your mind that your parents said, your friends said, family members said " *you were always like that*" you weren't good in: math, musically inclined, whatever, you fill in the _____.

Stop, right now.

"*Think it through*" Change it by practicing positive self talk.

I have a conscious choice right now, how I want to respond to a situation. It's my attitude. It's my Life. It's my own "Self Talk".
I choose.

When a comment or statement is made about you, not in a positive or constructive manner, stay focused. Look nicely and pleasantly at the messenger and smile when the speaker is stating an opinion about you not based on reason or reality. Your internal self talk might go something like this: "You don't know me at all, or understand me even a little bit. I am so much bigger than your misunderstood comment."

Your opinion of yourself, your self concept is what really counts. I get to choose how to respond, in a positive, productive manner each time, every time. Don't let anyone knock you off your centre.

How high is your altitude on your attitude?

Realize right now, today and tomorrow, someone else's opinion or comment on you, your skills, your ability, your whatever, is nothing but a temporary thought in time and space that has no bearing whatsoever unless *you allow it to!*

We all have thousands and thousands of thoughts everyday.
The most important ones, are the positive ones moving yourself, your life, your goals forward followed by ACTION NOW!

Your attitude, your opinion, your comments, your internal talk is what counts and is paramount.
Talk it up, jazz it up, and make it up - your mind. All this can move your life forward when you have thought about it, a little while longer. Believe, energize, and emotionalize to realize your life forward, how you want it be.
No one can define you and put parameters on you, or mental shackles, only if you let them.

KEY
Remember - Realize that everything counts in your life!
This idea by being more positive with a "definiteness of purpose" is so important to get a handle on every day.
All that really matters is to realize that right now, this moment this second that you are becoming more aware, and that moving your life forward in every aspect is what is most important.
Every action, thought, word, and deed, choice, "your choices" brought you to exactly the spot you are present today: good, great, bad, indifferent or incredible! You are continually a summation of your thoughts, desires, decisions, actions & inactions.

Am I off track a bit, with some of my habits? We all are, have been, and like a rocket ship on its' course, we need to keep "self-correcting" towards our goals and destinations.

Let's get back on track. It's never too late. Start all over.
Am I eating too much, drinking too much, and not exercising enough?
Slow down, cut down, and get into a new groove.
It's really up to you. When? How? You know why?

Your attitudes can change. Your not so healthy habits can change. We all have them, you are not alone.

"Manage your weaknesses and develop your strengths" Bob Proctor

Learn from Life.
Learn from yourself.
Learn from others.

You can learn from the mistakes of others if you're more aware and observant.

You don't have to make the same mistakes that other people make for you to learn valuable lessons. Think about it! Learn from the best and from the worst! Model your success from formulas that are working for other people in health, wealth, and positive personal development.

Personally I am a student of constant learning, reading and perpetual self-improvement because I want to and experience more of what life has to offer. What floats your boat? What rocks your world? What have you always wanted to do, try, really, what is it? Go for it! Raise your sails, chart your course. It only takes a couple of ingredients:

Write it down, think about it, take actions steps towards it, set a date, list the advantages and challenges in advance, and adjust your action plan along the way. That plan worked for Walt Disney, should work for you too! (☺)

You can learn something, about almost anything from the worlds' libraries, universities, educational TV programs, social media, radio, movies and the wonderful world of the internet. All have unique forms of knowledge in them from every conceivable scope of the human imagination thus far.

The Good, The Bad, The Ugly, The Beautiful, The Triumph, The inspirational, The Powerful, The Divine, The Mind, The Infinite, The List goes on! It is up to you to pursue your own personal advancement. What do you want to create? What do you want to will yourself to become?

Learning never stops. Never stop learning!

Your mind continues to grow and learn if you want it to, exercise it to, will it to.

Your level awareness continues to grow, if you want it.

Your understanding continues to grow if you want it.

How good do you want it all – various aspects of your life?

Re-Alignment

What is my purpose?_Is my purpose on purpose?

Am I aligning myself with the right ideas, right people, right situations that might move myself in the right direction? Do I want to make changes in my life? When, if not now, when?

Do I have every situation, every part of my life in the right order, ideal state, under control?

Can I stand myself or others?

Am I holding people, family and friends up to unrealistic standards or ideals and when they fall short, I feel let down, or disappointed? Am I judging them from my standard? Do I do that to myself? Am I projecting, "The why aren't they doing something better about themselves," syndrome? Look in the mirror first. ☺

Love – Forgive – Sorry – Thankful- Move Forward – Be Unconditionally Accepting - Carry On!

Where is my alignment? In an ancient adage from Socrates one of the great Greek philosophers of ancient time's states; "***Know Thy Self***" and I would personally add, *__"Never stop knowing yourself and what you are capable of becoming and creating in the world. The world needs you."__*

Ready Set Action!

Action: the state of moving forward, an act of will.
- Act: a state of real existence rather than a possibility.

How is your state of being of possibilities developing?
Are you acting upon your goals, your changes, your desires to be truly that which you are meant to be? Are you directing your life or are you being directed by circumstances? Does the media, your family, your friends, your school, your fellow employees, your employer or your own negative self talk constantly influence you?
Well, stop it!
Right now make a decision to live your life by your design, not by default.

Do you ever spend a few seconds thinking about someone and then you're off on another thought trip?

What's so important in your life is what is affecting and influencing you.

We all get caught up sometimes in *"what we will they think"* more than actually valuing our own thinking. Your life could be rough, in shambles going down in flames and the people who know you, love you, are so caught up in their own lives, own concerns, they might give a quick thought to your situation, then think, about how many toppings should I order on tonight's pizza.

That's life sometimes, eh!

Here are some examples of random thoughts to illustrate the point.
"What do I have to pick up again after work, on the way home?"
"I hope I'm not late for my hair appointment."
"The baby needs diapers, good game on this weekend."
"The car needs an oil change that light keeps coming on."
"I'll do the wash tomorrow."
"I just want to relax tonight and watch a good movie."
"I have to take the kids to hockey"
"I think I saw the neighbors lost puppy, down the street."

"I hope I can get my life back on track."

"What should I make for dinner tonight?'

"I need to talk to my friend about the party, what should I wear, whose going anyways?"

"There is too much construction going on, it takes way to long to finish."

"I was a bit harsh with the kids today."

"I need to start loosing weight again; these jeans are getting snug."

"Why doesn't so and so call me anymore?"

"My goal is to save up enough money for that trip, we want to go on."

Get the picture; see what's going on with people and their continuous flows of thoughts.

I have heard that educated scientists and psychologists approximate that we all have thousands and thousands of thoughts a day. The point here is that are brain is constantly thinking.

Stop worrying and wasting time thinking about; what other people think about you. If you are placing more value on what other people are thinking about you than yourself, it's time to develop a positive mindset for yourself.

I am all for setting a good example to family, friends, community and the global village at large in all that we do and the actions we take. (Just for the record)

Thoughts are fleeting within seconds of time.

Control your thoughts, your thinking and value your thoughts.

Become more aware of your thoughts with a conscious effort. How are you thinking about things? What patterns and paradigms are you operating on?

Change your thinking by conscious intention. How good do you want it to be, today and tomorrow?

It's not easy, but it's worth the effort to make conscious change in any area of your life.

Don't worry about trying to change every area or every paradigm in your life at once. You have to develop the habits, the skill to do so; you have to have good fortitude, courage, will power and perseverance. We all can do it, one area at a time.

Some thought patterns run on paradigms and conditions of habit over the years that seem ingrained and have always been that way. They too can be changed; "*this too shall pass*," if you want it to.

"I've always been that way" "I can never loose weight"

"He's so stubborn, so negative, such a bore"

Go ahead try to erase those statements in an instant, after they have been played, heard, repeated, re-enforced by self or others over the years.

It's not easy at first, but like messages on your phone, it can be recorded over.

Be conscious of the fact, that any conditioning or reinstating something more positive over something negative can be accomplished through positive repetition. Being consistent is one key in everything.

You can replace any bad habit with a good habit. It takes anywhere from 21 to 30 days depending on the habit. The magic number is inside of you. When self talk habits, that have been negative over the years, they can take longer, however, is it not worth to change your conditioning for the better?

You can, by the way of a consistently having a positive mindset to perceive the world as you would like it to be.

Re-condition your thinking to what, how, why you want to change, be your best, and move your life forward, not backward and not stay the same.

Your thoughts make you or break you, condition you positively or negatively. Fact.

Whether you believe this or not, just look around you and see how each and every individual on the planet is a reflection of their thoughts, their inner world, and their belief about themselves. They are what they are thinking about, attracting about, believing about, expecting about, and feeling about.

We all have the same 24 hours, similar body; we all have a brain/mind conscious of our life expression. The differences between us is our levels of awareness and the results we are shaping our lives by our thoughts, actions and inactions to a greater or lesser extent.

Think about that for a moment.

Our Level of awareness = Action = Results.

How aware do you want to become? How much action do you want? (No pun intended)

How much do you want to change the course of your life and get better results in your life, right now?

"How Great Do You Want It!?"

The number one thing, #1, numero uno, you must realize today and everyday, all the great thinkers have said it throughout the ages; you must have absolute clarity about what you want, really want and know your goal(s) and begin to achieve them.

What are you willing to give up, sacrifice for, what you really want for today and tomorrow?

What is your life statement?

What is the legacy you are developing and are going to leave behind along with your great name?

Time and time again great people, leaders, from humble beginnings to celebrated lives have had this in common: a crystal clear, sense of purpose, and clarity of their goals, what they want to achieve and do. They were able to move their lives in the direction of "how good they wanted it." We all experience our lives emotionally, physically, intellectually and spiritually. How good do we want our relationships, personally and professionally? I think the material good comes as a by-product in the spirit of giving back as naturally as, a better way to live and create.

You choose how you feel most of the time. You choose the right action, attitude and alignment most of the time, or not. Always remember, it's OK to keep putting yourself back on track, change the habit, start again and begin again.

"It doesn't matter where you've been, it only matters where you are right now and where you are going." Brian Tracy

"Success is the progressive realization of a worthy ideal or goal. **Earl Nightingale, one the first great** *radio broadcaster in the personal development fields.*

Challenge your clarity. If it stands up to the test, make action plans and stay in hot pursuit! Small goals lead to progress, bigger goals leads to greater skills and development and greater progress. When you accomplish a goal, do it on a small scale first; it will reinforce your new habits, and it will give you mental energy and commitment to keep building a momentum towards what's next, what's possible!

Hey, my life is by my design, my intent, my doing, and my making it happen! My way!

How good, great do I really want with all the clarity and responsibility of my own personal awareness taking shape to help mould the future, my future, my family's, the world?

Being consistent is **Key!**

No matter what endeavor, goal, habit to change, and new habits to form, being consistent is a paramount key.

Personally I used to be *"consistent at being in-consistent"* Start, stop, begin, pause, lose weight put it back on. Start, fail – "diet starts Monday." I'll start writing more tomorrow, on the weekend, the new exercise routine starts. When the weekend is over, I'll get back on track, right after our vacation, as soon as the birthdays pass, anniversary, summer party, thanksgiving, Christmas, in the New Year. Sound familiar? I have said all those statements.

I have been to "some day I'll" so many times.

Until I decide to vote myself off some day I'll/Island. (Pun intended)

Lots of people are there on "some day I'll" get around to doing something, making that change.

I know friends, family members, habits, attitudes and paradigms all playing on the same roller coaster of "maybe one day."

"Some day I'll" is a comfortable cozy place, a comfort zone of the many not the few!

"Vote yourself off of someday I'll"   **Denise Waitley**

Start right now, today, this hour, this minute, this second!

Know that everything counts, it all matters, everything is important, everything.

How important is your day, your life, where you stand with your spouse, your family, your employer, your team, your employees and your business?

How good do you want your life statement, your true sense of purpose?

Is your purpose on purpose? Is what you are doing, how you are living truly the way you want it to be? Again, remember you are exactly where you are today, by the sum accumulation of all your thoughts, desires, actions and inactions. Awareness thus far, like it?

There have been a few repeat lines in this book, I know, it's intentional. I wanted it that way, its worth repeating and re-reading. I don't know about you but for me, it takes a couple of repeats, reads and life lessons to sink in through my think skull. Thank you for reading my book thus far.

I am honored and happy and grateful for the privilege to share with you some of my personal thoughts and life lessons.

Control, you are in control, you have to realize the more control you take over your thoughts, the better clarity you have, the more clarity, the better results you can achieve by taking control over your thoughts, the way you think about things. You have the right and responsibility to control everything you think about.

Clearer Notes:

_____

_____

_____

_____

_____

_____

_____

_____

CHAPTER 4

Time Today Tomorrow

Webster's New Collegiate Dictionary Definition
Time: *"a continuum which lacks spatial dimensions and in which events succeed one another from past through present to future. Oxford: the unlimited continued progress of existence and events in the past, present and future, regarded as a whole."*

"Does anyone really know what time it is?" Line from a Chicago song. ☺

Everyday, everywhere everyone has the exact same amount of time. 24 hours, 1,440 minutes, 86,400 seconds no more no less.
Time is the great equalizer for everyone. How well do you spend your time?

Do these statements sound familiar?
"I don't have enough time."
"There is never enough time."
"I don't have time for this or that."
"We are just wasting time."
"I was just killing time."

"We had the time of lives."
"How much time do we have?"
"We were just in time."
"You're wasting your time with that."
"Are you having the time of your life?"

The time is now! How good is your time?
Take time seriously. What is done is done, your past, good, great, grateful, pathetic, poor, or prosperous.

It's all been a result of your thinking, directly or indirectly.
It doesn't matter in one sense, at one time, where you've been. What matters the most right now is the time you are presently in, what you are doing right now and are you moving towards a progressively fulfilling future? The continuous action toward worthy ideals and goals, your worthy goals are what counts now.
Your time is now! Get off the bench and the sidelines and be in the biggest "game" of your life!
You are the Master "Time Maker" of your life.
It's true, look around you: what has been done, is being done, and will be done by people taking their "time" into their own hands perceptions of reality and just making it count.
I believe everything counts in every way every day be it a gesture, smile, positive thought, and an action towards your goal. You can take small steps, then bigger steps, faster, greater and grander steps.

How much time do you want to put into changing your life, your family, your community, your nation, your world for the better?

I personally believe if everyone would realize, how important their own life is, and how it is linked to everyone else's in some cosmic/quantum way, even greater accomplishments could be realized and mutual understandings of all persons on the planet be maintained. Isn't it about time?

What do most people want: health, happiness and harmonious ways of living: peace of mind, right?

If you go just about your day, just existing in semi-unconscious thinking, then "wake up my friend." Live your life, your life by design, not by default.

Remember we have lots of habits and mindsets, mental blueprints of our self image.

The time is now to enhance your self image of your health, wealth, weight, work, athletic ability, success and everything else you want to develop.

Change the image, change your thoughts, change your actions = changed results, direction and alignment. Do you have time to make that change? It's easier than you think! Take one area of your life, you are presently unsatisfied with and start there.

Manage your weaknesses, until you become a little bit better in the area of self improvement. Here is a little known fact: once you start to improve in just one area of your life; it starts to have a compound effect on others areas as well in a positive way just by association of change taking place. Stop beating yourself up, stop negative self talk on every level.

The human body, mind, spirit is one of the most unique expression life forces in the universe. We are conscious of that great fact! From the times of the caveman to the International Space Station, we are all thinking on different levels of awareness and exploration.

The more you become aware of your own thinking and belonging, the thoughts you are thinking, the more "control" you will have over every and any circumstance. The more you feel you have control over your life, the more peace of mind can be experienced.

Great mindsets take time to realize and develop.

Is that worth all the time in the world? The more you become aware, the more time you spend in making your life, your conditions, circumstances to benefit yourself, and others in a positive way. Isn't that a great thing to do, and to never give up or stop trying?

Isn't it about time we all get crystal clear on our own right thinking?

The time is now, not tomorrow, not the "diet starts Monday or after the holidays!"

Have faith in yourself, have faith in others, and "have faith" in humanity!

I do, it's worth it! The great Nazarene taught us centuries ago about how important it is to have faith. Faith works wonders! Today Matters!

All we have is today, right now, what we are becoming, doing, thinking, not becoming, not doing, *"how good do you want today to be!?"* Tomorrow will come after today. Today is the day, your day! You might be experiencing the results of many yesterdays today. Remember and realize exactly where you are today is a result of your thinking, your actions and inactions of times past.

You will always see, feel, and be today as a result of times past of your thinking and actions.

Tomorrow will be today's seeds planted deep in the mind of your thought garden.

What are you growing, weeds,… or planting seeds of wonder, life expressions, goals and ideals of worthy accomplishment, peace and prosperity, friendship and fun and where you want to be?

Thought Notes:

_____

_____

_____

_____

_____

_____

_____

_____

CHAPTER 5

Involvement Imagination Intention

How **involved** are you really about taking complete responsibility for your own life?

Are you consciously involved or are you going through the motions?

Everyone is in constant motion, you - me, we are all involved in an expression of life that is far deeper than our present understanding.

Being involved in your conscious decisions will free you up to do, think, act and be more than your present situation and awareness. Don't let present circumstances dictate what you're capable of doing or changing. Get more involved. Any earnest effort towards your participation reaps the rewards. Be seriously involved about taking better care of yourself, mentally, physically, emotionally, spiritually, intellectually, socially, and globally. Don't feel like getting involved from your comfort zone or being a back bencher, stop, the world needs you! Get involved and make motions, make mistakes, make'em talk. Do it right, do it scared, do it invigorating, and do it for yourself. Every action has a reaction and every cause has an effect.

As **Nike** says: *"Just do it!"*
What a great mantra!

Imagination

Do it imaginative. Do it your way!
Do you think, Walt Disney, Bill Gates, Oprah, Donald Trump, Gretzky, Mozart, Michelangelo, Socrates, and Aristotle did it with imagination?
There are millions more with the same mind like yours and mine.
They all do it by believing, creating, and imagining something, an idea bigger themselves.
What image were they holding onto in their minds?
What is the "true image" you want for your life?
How Good Do You Want It to be?
If you can imagine it, if you want your life differently, you can have it by impressing that thought image to take shape and form first in your mind. It doesn't happen in an instance, but by being consistently conscious of what you want and are thinking about imagined to come about in your reality.

If I really want something, with passion, emotion, courage and confidence all under the umbrella of having an attitude of gratitude, it begins to happen, not in an instant but in its' right time. If I believe and expect, I will attract, if I put out the right intentions and work on being my best. I must always take the necessary action steps towards the goals and life, I am seeking to attain.

Imagine here right now, how good you want your life to be.
What does it look like? Make an image impact, an impression of how you want it to be really, and truly. Be involved, be imaginative, and be the impact you want on the world, your world, our world.

KEY: By constantly holding onto that unique image every day, every time we get a conscious chance, it moves us one step closer to the desired reality more or less. Thoughts are forms of energy that can crystallize and materialize into ideas of substance reality.

Intention

By having right intentions, good intentions and thoughtful forward intentions, I believe things in life will align themselves for you. We all have good intentions. When we don't have the right or best intentions for something or towards someone else, things usually don't turn for the best, right?

The universe is really on your side. Intend well, be well, ask well, and *"all shall be given to you, seek and you will find, knock and the doors of awareness will be opened to you." Paraphrased from the Bible.*

"What are your good intentions?"

Towards your health:

_____

_____

_____

_____

_____

_____

_____

_____

Towards your wealth:

_____

_____

_____

_____

_____

_____

_____

_____

Towards you learning something new:

_____

_____

_____

_____

_____

_____

_____

Notes:

_____

_____

_____

_____

_____

_____

_____

_____

CHAPTER 6

Optimism Observation Order

Optimism: an inclination to put the most favorable construction upon actions and events or to anticipate the best possible outcome.

Pessimism: an inclination to emphasis achieve, aspects conditions, and possibilities or to expect the worst possible outcome.
(Both definitions from the Webster's New Collegiate Dictionary)

How do you want to interpret your life with the results you are getting?
Your mind is very powerful, thoughts and ideas are one of the purest forms of energy. Ask any scientist.
Your thoughts can be directed to help form your reality, your life.
Yes, you are responsible, nobody else, not the government, not society, not your culture, which by the way is a form of "group think" customs. When you think of your life, what it is, what it could be, what you could make it to be, and what your attitude is about everything it is really up to you.

(Thought)
What new habits am I willing to do, make, to change my life for how I truly want it to be?

One must realize we live in three realms of existence at the same time. Physically in our bodies. (mostly water by the way) ☺
Intellectually: our "one" mind.
Spiritually, the life force which moves us and is in us.
Life is always for fuller expression and expansion. This dynamic trio is embedded with our emotions as human beings.
We are responsible; we have a conscious choice to exercise all these faculties for better or for worse.
How physically fit do you want to be?
How much mental will power do you want to exercise?
How much faith do you have, in yourself, in humanity, yes, even in God?

For my "non" believers in a God, you can use "higher power" first cause if you will, first mover and shaker, prima movem. What's in a name? (☺)

Try this:
Take your left or right hand and with your index finger move it closer to the other hand without touching it and start to make a circular motion around the inside of the palm of that hand slowly and steadily. You will feel a force or personal energy. You are alive with a motion of energy that can neither be created nor destroyed.

I'm optimistic, are you?

Observation

How well are you observing your life?
What do you take into account about the results you are presently getting right now?

It is easy to say, "Well that's just the way things are."
"It's always been like this or that way," Says who?
When we observe, honestly observe ourselves, our situations, we come to realize by the way of noted facts, the continuance of experience in our lives is a result of all our decisions both conscious or not.
Now the great thing we can learn about ourselves or a situation is from first hand experience and or the observations, actions, mistakes and successes of others.

If you want different and better results in your life, observe what other people are doing, did, have done, and follow, mirror or lead through the way from others' successes! It's easier than you might think.
You can do anything someone else has done.
The human potential factor far out-weighs all self limiting beliefs that are cast in front of it.
Observe and realize, yes if it's up to me, I am going to make my life all that I can possibly be.
Make it count!
  Make it work!
  The time is now, not manana/tomorrow not later, not next
  Monday, not when I get a round tuit.
  It is now! You know that time is the great level playing field.
  How we leverage our time, how we observe what needs to
  be changed, or done is always ongoing.

This process never stops, for we are either being people who create and relate or disintegrate and deflate.
Observe this, the choice is yours!

Order

One has to continually bring their life to order. How much order would you say you life is in, on every front? Where there is order, there is clarity, where there is clarity; there is a consciousness of purpose. What do you really want? Who do you really want to be? Do you want order, how do I get out of chaos to order? Well, that might depend on how good you want it, not just for a day but a life time.

The conscious choice is yours today and tomorrow.

You can start anytime, start from where you are, try to bring one aspect of your life to super order and then move onto the next.

It's really that simple. One step at a time, one small change at a time, one difference is all it takes to get started on the road to more order. The more you have order in your life, the more you have control. The more order and control increases your self esteem. The more self esteem you have, the more self confidence you will have. The confidence of the self engages more opportunities to enhance the expression of your life. Greater expression of your life enhances other people's experience of life as well. We all need each other to keep moving forward with a momentum of persistence, passion and purpose.

Can I take your order? ☺

Notes:

_____

_____

_____

_____

_____

_____

_____

_____

CHAPTER 7

Now Negativity Never

Now

The present time is now. The **time** is now.
Do not wait until all conditions and circumstances are just right to begin your life changing goals.
Just do it now, today.
Why wait? For what? Until you feel like it? I think the world would be a different place if everyone just did what they had and only when they "felt" like it. One of the differences between successful people and unsuccessful people is that, more successful people do the things that have to be done, discipline themselves, even when they don't feel like doing them.

Lots of folks want to wait until things are just right, the right time, the right place, or tomorrow, this weekend, next meeting, next Monday.
I will start the diet, the project after the holidays, after Thanksgiving, as soon as we get through this quarter, after Christmas, the start of the New Year, after the Super Bowl, after my birthday, once school starts, this spring, this summer.

We all do it, every one of us. I still do it! We can always put something off and procrastinate until next time, next event, and next celebration.

WHY? The time is now, not "O whenever."

Negativity: to negate, to say no, to deny, to deny the existence or truth of something. To cause to be ineffective or invalid, nullify- to make of no value or consequence.
(Webster's N.C.D.)

How negative some people are, eh? Why is that so? Is being more positive better for you than being negative? Your personal health is one of your score cards. Are positive people healthier than negative people? Yes they are, mentally and physically.

I know and believe there is more good, and what's "right" with the world than all the areas we all need to improve upon.

Remember your attitude, your choice of thoughts, thinking and being, enhances your experience of life, reality and what and how you choose to see the world, relations, realities and responses to how you are being.

You are part of the world, the world needs you. The world needs your voice, your song, your inventions, your creations, your music, your magic, your willingness to serve and take care of others that need it most, your positive ideas, your presence, your purpose, your passion, your positivity.

Never

The word never has the letter "n" in front of it. When we remove the n, we get ever. When we join the word ever to other words, we get some great words: everlasting, evermore, every time, everywhere every day, evergreen. Every thought counts. ☺

The universe is constantly expanding in every direction, everyday. It never stops. Energy never stops morphing from one form into another. The vibration of your being is constantly in motion. Life is constantly ever being and changing. It's good, it's all good. This mystical first cause of life exists. Gravity exists whether we believe it or not. There are natural laws in the universe that govern every aspect of our lives whether, we are aware of them or not. I think that is why science keeps going deeper into the world of atoms and quantum physics as well as out to the depths of space further into the cosmos to explore and better understand our universe and ourselves.

I believe.

I believe in you!

Do you believe in you?   I believe, always have and always will!

Never, ever, give up today or tomorrow my friend. There is so much in life to know and explore.

The world needs you.

What are some of your beliefs?

Do they challenge you or stifle you?

Excite you and doubt you?

Notes:

_____

_____

_____

_____

_____

_____

_____

_____

CHAPTER 8

NEW

When we become aware of something new, we tend to get excited by this new realization, this new understanding, of a law, fact, figure, and truth. Now, what do we do with it? Keep moving your awareness level forward, every day in every way. Never stop learning and becoming into being, more aware, more understanding, more knowledgeable. I believe we are human beings more than just human doings. What you think your life should look like is up to you to move it, think it in that direction.

You are responsible, now, today and tomorrow. It's really that simple on a daily basis. Put yourself into this new awareness with your full heart, not half a heart. What are you trading the days of your life for, because we trade our time, our hours, minutes and seconds everyday? Does watching more TV, bring more meaning to my life? All things are good in there correct proportion to right thinking, right attitude, right development towards enhancing and engaging ones' life into a more profound sense of being aware. *Aristotle* always said, *"Moderation in all things."*

What's New in your thinking right now?

Jot it down:

Notes:

_____
_____
_____
_____
_____
_____
_____
_____
_____

CHAPTER 9

(A mini exploration of thinking about every thing)

Omnipresent

Omnipresent: present in all places at all times.
Omniscience: is having infinite awareness, understanding and insight into all things, laws of the universe. (Webester's NCD)

The thoughts, ethers and energy of the entire universe are omnipresent in all things at all times, I believe. All great ideas have been around forever just waiting for the human mind to make them into a realization. We become aware of possibilities when collectively, we've worked towards them as goals to be achieved. The knowledge of the wheel was around during the caveperson days as was the automobile, the light bulb, learning how to fly in a plane, and now we are in space. The telephone, radio, internet have always existed; it wasn't until of recent that the human minds, desired a progressive realization for its awareness to come into existence. The individuals, who dared to think differently, use their imagination and faculty of creative thinking developed these remarkable ideas into reality. We have all stood on the shoulders of giants, great thinkers and the advancement of technology to get and become, where we are today.

Our desire for constantly improving peoples' lives on the planet warrants creative ideas to explore and made into reality by our collective and individual thinking.

Think about it. How can we improve upon an idea, a way of doing things better, and differently than before, by way of a collective mindset and limited understanding of times past? As we educate ourselves, the planet all peoples, the unfolding growth of educated minds, thinkers and believers of what is possible will continually and exponentially come into reality.

How good do we want it, for everybody, not just a few?

Nature has a great way of keeping all things into perspective by its true value of its life cycles. Everything grows, sheds, replenishes, rebuilds and keeps moving forward. We are all in it, this life, together.
Know the nucleus of your thoughts and how they are affecting the way you think, feel and are right now. You are a part of it all.
How Good Do You Want It!?
How do you really want to be?
Do you ever say that's not the real "me" or "I'm not really like that?"
"You haven't seen the real me."
Be Now! Be yourself, whether or not, you fully realize it.
Isn't life a wonderful continuum of unfolding, discovery, and becoming more aware of an omnipresent in your life?

Living a lifetime in a day!
Do you "carpe diem" = "seize the day", or wait and wish until the day is over?
This is your day, today, you can consciously choose what you want to think, self talk, feel about, regret about, pity me about, and it is really up to you.

Are you creating the circumstances you want, or at least looking for them and or becoming the progressive realization of what it is you want, really want? One step, one earnest effort a day builds on, builds up that thought impulse into desire, into action, into reality, day by day. Be open, be smart, be what you want to be. You're unique, there isn't nor can than ever be someone exactly like you. That's an impressive thought to carry around. There can only be, one just like me. Believe to be your personal best every day in every way. The laws of being will conspire to be with you, guide you, prompt you, and encourage you today, tomorrow, and together. It's real, it's now, and it's unique and wonderful. Plus, again remember, we are all in it together. No one is ever truly alone. There might be times, episodes and situations when we feel that state of aloneness, but, is it really a unique oneness we haven't fully come into being with, a different type of an awareness? I don't know. I put that thought idea out there, because it came to me while writing this chapter.

Omni Notes:

_____

_____

_____

_____

_____

_____

_____

CHAPTER 10

Winner   Wisdom   Waiting

What defines a **winner**? I like the definition: one that is successful especially through praiseworthy ability and hard work.

What are you trading the days of your life for? Are you winning or really just beginning?

Babe Ruth was a home run hitter king in days past, also a strike out king.

Michael Jordan scored the most free throws in his day, and also missed the most.

Thomas Edison had 1000s of failures before he finally got it right to create the incandescent light bulb. Michael Schumacher is one of the greatest racers of all time; in how many races do you think he didn't place first? Steve Jobs always thinks big from Apple. He is following what he is passionate about.

Mario Andrettie became great in auto racing by never giving up and lived to race again and again.

Nelson Mandela never gave up on what he truly believed in and always had hope. Mother Theresa showed the world great love, by one act of kindness every day for a life time.

Is your life in a constant forward motion, challenging thinking, thinking a little bit better, a little bit bigger?

Walt Disney during his early days said he was always "18 months away from bankruptcy". They still have undeveloped plans of his dreams and visions, today.

What is your vision? What legacy are you working on?

My own personal RV sales record is one of the greatest in South Western Ontario; I've also had the most people to say "no" as well! That's Life.

I keep moving myself forward.

The odds are always in your favor: the more "no's" failures, misses, losses, you have, the closer you become to your successes, triumphs and goals to be accomplished.

One of the truest secret to all things is to never, ever give up, give in or feel it's not worth it.

Remember, everything counts, everything is worth it, everything impacts, impresses everything else to a greater or lesser extent.

Yes, How Good Do You Want It!?

People always remember you for your achievements, your successes, turning your life around, getting back on track, getting on the right track, what you are doing now, making now, creating now. Use all you mistakes as seeds of experience to your successful endeavours.

Right Now! Right On!

Wisdom: *an accumulated philosophic or scientific learning; knowledge, ability to discern inner qualities and relationships; insight, good sense judgment. A wise attitude on a course of action.*

Wise: *a characterized by wisdom; marked by deep understanding, keen discernment and capacity for sound judgment. B; exercising sound judgment; prudent a knowing.* (***Webster's NCD***)

I may not be a wise man at times; however, I am wising up to becoming more aware in my life about a lot of things constantly, by choice and so can you. It is always good to keep asking the "whys" in your life. Is your personal "WHY" big enough to move you forward towards the life you want and intend it to be?

Any new awareness that comes about from thinking, reading, discussing is worthwhile. New means something that has come into existence in a short time, something that has not been known before.

For example: The universal laws of gravity, attraction, expectancy, cause and effect have always existed, but when one becomes aware of them, they are "new" to that person.

Something old can be new. Something ancient can be newly discovered.

Something now understood is "new" to a mind, your mind, your awareness and mine.

Developing a constant positive attitude and a thirst for learning can affect every aspect of your life if you are open to the discipline of it.

Neutral: *not engaged on either side, not electrically charged, a position of disengagement.* (Webester's NCD)

Tired of being neutral then neutralize your neutral-ness in all things.

Your heart is not neutral. Your mind is not neutral. Your emotions are not neutral in and of themselves.

I think it is better to be positive and have loved more than have waited all your life, taken that risk, jumped in with both feet, asked to, said yes to, ventured onto, climbed onto, swam across, invested time into, and taken action towards goals, ideas, relationships and opportunity to, more life.

To live a life and then realize at a certain point, you ask yourself: "What If!? If I only would have, had, done, tried, believed, risked, asked, loved, moved, studied, traveled, said, adapted, adopted, accepted, spoken to, spoken at, volunteered for, believed in him, her, them, us, me, we,--
Your call!
Your move! Your step! Your destiny! Your Life!
How do you want it to be!?
This is your time, your life, and your 24 hours today, every day in every way.

Do I want to really see what's going on?
Do I want to really believe, if it's meant to be, it's up to me?

It's always better to be crystal clear about what you want in your life and the direction you are moving.
If you have a goal that moves you forward, challenges you side ways, then Just Goal for it!
Make it personal, make it unique. Make it what you want it to be, not someone else's expectation.
Make your goal yours, because you want it to be!
Be yourself. Be your best, every day in every way and always remember everything "counts."
You need to move your life, your thoughts in the direction you desire. Your thoughts are significant forces towards the development of your present and future.

Do not let your present circumstances "think you" into this is all there is, it's was meant to be, it's my plight; it's that way it has been.

Take Flight, to new heights, your heights my friend. Today is the beginning of a new day: own it, make it yours, the world needs that you be all you can.

How Good do You Want to Be!?

You are needed, wanted, hoped for, looked up to, your are one of God's greatest miracles of creation, in case you haven't been told that lately. You are! Now you know, never forget that.

To live by the Golden rule and "treat everyone in the world how you want to be treated," we will all change our world for the better.

What is the best solution, for this situation, person, business, and team?

What matters most to you, right now is where you are headed, where you are going in the right positive mindset of right thinking. It is paramount to believe this and take this to heart.

The world needs you to be right on track and keep getting back on track.

The past is the past, nothing can be done to change it - so - if there were lessons to be learned there, great big ones, small ones, harsh ones, so be it. Accept it, embrace it, and move on, and keep moving forward.

The "**Key**" to very successful people, is that they have a constant state towards action not stagnation.

Are you deciding to move your life forward, because your heart is in a constant beat of right rhythm, right thinking, right on, on the right track?

Deep down inside, you know when something is right. If you have formed any habits that are counter productive to a right rhythm of living and right thinking, consciously choose to start changing them now. One at a time, one day at a time.

Once you get a momentum started, an excited sense of being on purpose starts to unfold within.

Make your purpose on purpose. We are all in this together. We all need each other and influence each other. I need the best from you and you can expect the best from me. When I make a mistake, fail, I keep getting myself back on track and "do" again. *"There is no try, just do."* Yodi –Jedi Master Star Wars. ☺

I am doing the following to enhance, develop and create a more positive mindset with the various aspects of my Life:

_____

_____

_____

_____

_____

_____

_____

_____

CONCLUSION:
THIS IS GOOD!

You are a vessel my friend. You have within you the capacity for greatness.

The way you live your life, speaks volumes about what you are communicating to yourself, the world, the universe and everyone around you.

You are not alone; you are connected on many levels to the universe.

Where do you think you come from?

Why are you here on this magnificent planet orbiting around a star in an orderly universe that is continuously and constantly expanding?

You are part of it.

Biologically you know where you come from: a mother and a father.

How incredible life is that you are in it, meant to be in it and have something and many things to contribute to it on many levels.

You are an instrument of divine expression. You have something to give uniquely from your own point, moment in time.

Everything about you is significant. We are all creatures of habit for better or for worse. The choice is ours, everyday every time.

When you are persistent in a forward movement of positive action, everything begins to change. When you have a definite purpose, definite plans of action to "be the difference in the world" make it so.

How Good do You want it!?

A belief in what you want to happen, expect to happen, begins to create awareness for it to come into reality. When you are emotionally involved in *"good vibrations of life"* I think, the universe which is an ocean of motion and constant energy, it is expanding and expressing itself in and through you to some degree. The spirit of the divine. God's love.

Everything is unfolding exactly and precisely how it is suppose to be, right now, right here. You are exactly where you are by your thoughts and actions or inactions and your paradigms are playing out perfectly by law, by inevitability, there is an order to all things in the universe.

Is this how good you want it, your life?

You have the choice, the decision, and the right to make even more of your life, than what it is right now! Your Actions, Your Words, Your Thoughts, Your understandings.
You are free to decide, knowledge is power and when true understanding is applied properly towards the betterment of oneself and humanity that power of purpose makes all the difference in the world!

How Awesome Do You Want Your Life to Be!?

My Life Notes:

_____

_____

_____

_____

_____

_____

_____

_____

_____